This Much Endures

This Much Endures

John Purser

with an introduction by
Fiona Stafford

Kennedy & Boyd
an imprint of
Zeticula Ltd
Unit 13
196 Rose Street,
Edinburgh,
EH2 4AT,
Scotland.

http://www.kennedyandboyd.co.uk
admin@kennedyandboyd.co.uk

First published in 2021
Copyright © John Purser 2021

Introduction Copyright © Fiona Stafford 2021
Cover Image Copyright © Seán Purser 2021

ISBN 9781849212229 paperback

For Stewart Conn

Acknowledgements

Some of these poems have been published previously and of these some have since been revised.

Those under the heading *Ancient Voices* were originally commissioned for a scenario and script for the Malta International Arts Festival in 2019.

J. D. Fergusson "Glasgow Spring 1942" was published in *The Hunterian Poems* in 2015; *GLAHM 113597 – Lord Kelvin's "Pitch Glacier"* in *The Hunterian Museum Poems* in 2017.

Your Proffered Cheek appeared in *Autumn Voices*, 2018, as did *For Sheila In Memoriam Leslie Henderson* which was also published in *The Dark Horse*, issue 39, 2018.

Râg Shri in Glasgow was published in *Thali Katori*, 2017.

I am much indebted to Stewart Conn, Alan Riach and Fiona Stafford: they have advised on these poems, and Fiona Stafford has done me the honour of writing an Introduction to them.

My children, Seán and Sarah, have also been helpful, as has my wife, Barbara, who is the dedicatee of all the *Amoretti*.

The collection as a whole is dedicated to Stewart Conn, who has patiently and generously fostered and mentored my writing for nearly half a century.

Contents

Introduction

Fiona Stafford

'Raise the horns', 'Hear the ghosts of the cattle lowing' or a voice, 'leaving blossoms trailing from every wall'.

You cannot help but listen. And why would anyone turn down this volume? Here are poems of dedication, celebration, exhortation and invitation. Lucky the listener to be finding such company, such sense, such clarity, such joy. From first to last, the voice of the poems speaks with the economy of tested truth: utterly assured, utterly convincing. This is a man who knows, and what's more, a man who is glad to share. He could hardly be less like the last eccentric, whose tomb inspires one of the sequence of 'Dedications'.

John Purser's generosity of spirit is clear from the opening poem for 'Simon O'Dwyer at Sixty'. A birthday poem for a friend who specialises in historic musical instruments is an opportunity to celebrate his contribution to the world with a witty evocation of the ancient communities he has helped to keep alive. Instead of the usual glass, everyone is asked to 'Raise the horns /and never mind which end'. We might learn from O'Dwyer to play the ancient horns and trumpet his achievement or fill them with drinks and toast him instead. Whether toasting or trumpeting, what matters is 'the gift he gave, /and gives again'. Although the stirring lyric is a birthday gift, it is really a poem of gratitude, not just for O'Dwyer, but for Irish traditional music, for good craic, and for the perennial life and power of music itself. The poem is a 'Prelude' – a perfect introduction to a sequence of poems by a poet-composer-musician-historian.

Music runs through the entire collection, emerging in the rhythm of the lines, the verbal acoustics, the portraits of dancers, players, singers. Everywhere, music is making unexpected connections, as 'The Horses of Destiny' revolve in time to a nursery rhyme while those at 'Kerry Races' offer good and bad bets through the beat of their hooves. Even family debates are 'more like an old song' than an argument. John Purser understands, better than anyone, the eternal impulse to sing, to make music. From the early Irish people who turned the horns of dead cattle into musical instruments to the Pacific islanders, picking up empty shells, listening to the sea within or blowing out sorrow and exultation through their curling hollows, the instinct is universal. The twist of the conch, the curve of the horn reveal 'the same and simple law', as the opening sequence explores before 'The Bronze Age Horn' takes over to give its own take on the matter.

While this is a collection ready to give voice to objects in the ancient manner, it remains firmly footed on home ground. Cows may furnish instruments and inspiration for poet-musicians, but that does not stop them from being real, cud-chewing cows. Lest we should forget, the narrative 'MacCowan' brings home the tough existence of cattle and their keepers. John Purser writes books and composes music and lives as a crofter in Skye. He never fails to remember the origin of cow horns in coarse-haired, four-legged, feeling bodies. The 'long shapely horns' of his favourite cow are seen with a different kind of clarity from those that made ancient music: they are fondly recalled nevertheless for not touching the poet and his helpful neighbour as they battle to save a calf after a long, painful birth.

Elegies for beasts are long-established in Scottish literary tradition, but 'MacCowan' gives the old genre a distressingly modern twist. There is nothing humorous about the consequences of the legislation relating to the BSE outbreak, 'you must be slaughtered and buried', nothing sentimental about the haunting gaze of the deserted cow in the pen at Portree. The celebratory tone of so many of John Purser's poems is set against the profound bleakness of others. The volume's overall truth derives as much from the poet's understanding of the pain and injustice of the world as from his recognition of what helps to combat the darkness. A life-enhancing preoccupation with endurance depends on a hard-won sense of what is to be endured.

If the law of natural forms is simple, John Purser's poems are not. Theirs is, rather, a distilled clarity, in which anything extraneous has been left behind. The music of the poetry means that even if a detail is unfamiliar, we still trust its presence. There is no need to explain 'the voice of Hinemokemoke' because the poem tells us of ocean people, conch shells and a lonely girl. The reticence is essential to the tone and to the poem's power to linger in the mind. A biographical gloss on Simon O'Dwyer, or the various subjects of the Dedications, would be just as superfluous. We do not need to know the details of Dame Beryl Grey's distinguished career as a ballerina or her performance in *Donald of the Burthens,* to be moved by 'Your Proffered Cheek'. A poem composed by a musician with a long memory, dedicated to a ninety-year-old dancer who once took the role of Death speaks for itself. Nor is it necessary to have heard Prakriti Dutta to feel the effect of her voice. The poet's admiration for his subject is apparent at once from the tone and language of each poem, giving readers a sense of their great good fortune at being allowed into the relationship.

The self-disciplined selection of detail also helps to free the subjects. Alan Riach steps from the 21st century into the realm of legend as a 'doughty red-haired warrior' leading his companions with 'the sword of intellect' and words at once understated and inspiring 'What are you waiting for, lads?' Each poem carries a recognisable truth, while at the same time prompting readers to imaginative flight. 'RLS for Sarah' is the embodiment of the poet's art – a boat made of Skye green marble in the shape of a leaf, whose 'cargo is Imagination'.

A gift for narrative, evident in many of the poems, is inherent in John Purser's gift for friendship, which enables a kind of risk-taking protected by witty affection. His poem for Paddy and Fiona Bushe, 'The Storm of Decency', builds expectation brilliantly and reaches a surprising climax, before offering a retrospective reflection which invites us all to join in the laughter. Even when recounting an encounter with a stranger, as in 'After the Races', the same humane observation prevails until it all ends in a very memorable smile. The poet's engaging sense of his own more comical aspects is essential to his storytelling. The moving pair of sonnets dedicated to Michael Purser begin by thanking him for having to 'deal with being my Big Brother', before praising his patience, superior brain, unfailing support and capacity for sometimes being right. Readers are likely to feel that they are in the company not of the poet alone, but also his family and many friends.

Almost all the poems gathered here are love poems of one kind or another, whether relating to individuals, enthusiasms, places, animals, or humanity in general. At the heart of the collection are the 'Amoretti', in which the poet declares his love and gratitude for a life led in intimate companionship.   The sequence follows the numbers of the earlier 'Amoretti' published in *There is No Night*; readers of that collection will know not to expect the ghost of Spenser to be intruding on highly personal moments. Here we are privileged to hear the poet thinking of his wife 'squidged up' in bed like a hedgehog, emerging from the shower like a naiad, mending his favourite sweater or gracing the water of a mountain pool where reddening rowans offer afternoon shade.

These are rare poems of love, intensified by a consciousness of ageing and the dark thought that crosses the happiest of marriages – one day half of the partnership may be left to survive alone: 'We compete for which of us will be the first to die'. But time brings its own reward in the feelings that continue to deepen with every passing year.   'Birthday Suit' begins, 'When I first saw you... you were in your thirties', while in 'I know you will approve', the temporary absence of his life companion prompts the realisation that 'we have slipped into each other, /are each other's thoughts'. In 'The Green Dress', addressed even more directly to his wife, he observes that 'there's no need to speak. /So many words – so very many words /have flowed between us.' Yet still the words come. And we are so pleased that they do. 'Not a Sonnet' dwells explicitly on the limitations of language, the inadequacies of poetic form, but leaves us delighting in the flock of words as they fly beyond formal conventions in the exultant freedom of the fifteenth line.

'Amoretti XXIX: This Much Endures,' the title poem of the collection, moves from a book, a photograph and a childhood memory through personal loss and existential questions to a declaration of love. The closing lines, carefully qualified to ensure that any trace of Larkin is quickly washed away, say it all:

This is my love for you,
my kind companion of these several years,
and, insofar as anything survives,
this much endures.

This is an answer, too, to Spenser's gloomy observation in *Amoretti* Sonnet LVIII, 'for on earth nought hath endurance'. John Purser is well aware of ageing and decay. He is as forthright as

any Renaissance poet about the proximity of the grave. Still he expresses an unfailing faith in love in all its forms and in
Music from life,
Life from music

Fiona Stafford

ANCIENT VOICES

Prelude - for Simon O'Dwyer at Sixty

Raise the horns
and never mind which end:
blowing or drinking,
drinking or blowing,
this man deserves your energies.

Raise the horns,
and never mind the rules:
play it straight,
play it bent,
it must be winning in its ways.

Raise the horns
and never mind the grave:
music from life,
life from music,
that is the gift he gave,
and gives again.

There should be
apple blossom at his feet,
wild hares
dancing in attendance,
and there on the bough of an old thorn
a blackbird giving out
in celebration -
the one competitor
he will always have to take
into account.

I The Conch

From the sea, the sound of the sea.
the conch is an ear, a cochlea
listening to the ocean,
put it to your ear. Ear to ear.
Hear it sooth the song,
wind on wave-crests.

Never more alive than in death,
in death it has found its voice.
It calls across the waters of time,
a marvel of shell and air.

To the people of the sea it calls
to ocean people:
Maori Putatara, Pu Whakaoro,
Hindu Shankha, Peruvian Pututu,
Japanese Horagai, Sanskrit Sangu,
many are its names, sacred to all,
the trumpet of the god of the sea;
it is the first to command;
it is the ancestor of all trumpets.

Waves of sound spiral in its form
it is a shield of wind
it is the voice of Hinemokemoke – the lonely girl

worthy of worship
it can howl in sorrow
hoot in triumph.

It is the oldest of them all.
It is the ancestor of breath.

II The Cow Horns

All shapes obey the law.
Nothing grows but it must shape itself
to nature's own inevitable forms,
organic curvature and spiral cone,
bi-lateral symmetry, double helix,
call them what you will,
the conch and cow horn each obey
the same and simple law.

Torsion and curvature
maintained in constant proportion,
an osculatory kiss spread out in space
by growth in simple time.

Hear how the hollowed horns
clash, how the conch sounds in the shell of the horn.
Hear the ghosts of cattle lowing
through millennia, the herds of thousands,
thousands of years ago.

III The Bronze Age Horn

What is my story?
It is not simply told.
When molten metal
was poured into my mould,
the chaplets kept my core
evenly spaced, the conical curve
retained, untwisting
as the rich bronze alloy,
snaked into my form, expelling air
through the relieving vents
like steam from the nostrils
of a raging bull.

And then the sound: the purified sound
of a creative age far out into the west.
which spent more of its wealth,
time, energy, and ingenuity,
on music than on all things else.

I am no instrument of war,
to me – with me – you sing,
dancing for deities.
I am the sentence of the law
that man imposed on rock
refining the pulse
of the untiring forge.

I am the song of fire.

IV The Deskford Carnyx

Prolific pig, fertile ferocious omnivore
your heavy skull, brutal and thick
crushing the kernels of nuts
with powerful jaws, ridged palate, rock-like teeth
grinding matter with purpose
snuffling through the leaves of autumn
with sensitive snout
rooting up bulbs and truffles,
throat guttural with contented grunts.

Nocturnal lord, totemic animal of many clans
with hackles raised, a sharp comb,
harsh spinal hairs, the red eyes
coals of anger, lust and rage,
jaw, open, tongue, obtruded,
lifted aloft the heads of men;
and then the unearthly scream
from almost human vocal chords.
You know the conduct of death.
You too are one of us.

TWO HUNTERIAN POEMS

J.D.Fergusson "Glasgow Spring 1942"

Nineteen-forty-two: the war was at its worst, and you,
old artist, you were at your best: beauty your weaponry:
assurance of joy, brush-stroke, form,
tree, spire and figure in unified freedom.

Did you see the University tower
silhouetted against the blitz;
watch the incendiaries floating by
on their ominous parachutes?

Enough of that. It is spring.
Sunlight is indiscriminate –
and this fine figure of a lass,
her full breasts pressing proud
against her grape-red dress,
totally at ease,
poses for us all.

The trees have green shoulders:
her hair is flowers and fruit,
a dome inverts her chin;
her fingers form the angle of a roof,
assurance in the geometry of her arms.

Patches of white light brighten
everything, and the spire, piercing the top of the canvas,
disappears into space. As for the river Kelvin,
it would cut the painting in two,
were it not invisible.
But we know it is there, just as we know
the sky is not the limit
and spring is not just
capable of it, but has
invaded the entire land.

GLAHM 113597 – Lord Kelvin's "Pitch Glacier"

There is nothing more peaceful
than this silent experiment
a mahogany ramp
a lump of pitch
stretching itself
with almost infinite luxury
down the slope.

They say it's glacial
but glaciers break up, advance, retreat
almost as rapidly as armies
in a continental war.

Not so this staircase of
imperceptible pitch
sliding from note to note
down the scalar descent
gravitas gravitatum et omnia gravitas.

Pitch black from top
to bottom "cobbler's wax"
shattering like glass
under the hammer blow
but here
sliding ominously slow
like a sleepy snake

There is nothing more peaceful
than this silent experiment
yet it was designed to produce
turbulence.

Somewhere in Lord Kelvin's mind
the aether had form and substance
of a kind, and space was filled
with the currents of viscous tides.

The aether has vanished. How?
Into the aether. That's where aether goes.

But this inexorable flow
of darkness
challenges the darkness of our minds.

Solid or liquid, this calcified oil
could be as fractious
as shards of coal at the coalface,
as slippy and silent as honey
on a tiled floor.

And as for that turbulence
there is nothing so quiet
no experiment so secluded
no thought so protected
that it cannot be disturbed
by the insistences of life

the necessity of motion to matter.

"all matter duly formed is attended with signs of life."

Oh, Newton! Why did you retract?

And Kelvin, did you grasp
towards that reality
knowing that even space itself
must move?

AMORETTI

Amoretti OI - Easter Sunday

I think of you in bed squidged up
like a hedgehog under leaves.

Where I write, the two caged budgies
hold their heads backwards under their down,
one eye out of four kept open – though I don't suppose
they're looking for an Easter egg.

Were the great stone rolled, there should not be
in the whole disorder of creation one thing discovered
that has been harrowing hell these last three days.
You, the budgies, hedgehogs, you should all
have dreamt it out of existence long ago.

There is no stone to guard the tomb of all your sleeping:
if the cage were open, I doubt if the birds would go missing.
So, when you all unfurl in the morning, I hope
the only mad discovery will be
that we have love enough to keep us here
together in this gentle amity
where others would break all in breaking free.

Amoretti XXIV - The Green Dress

Wear your green dress for me
that you slip into so efficiently:
its gentle inward curves that follow yours,
its length implying
the smooth slenderness of your legs.

Wear your green dress for me
with my mother's opal necklace
round your neck, the amber
bracelet – wear that on your wrist:
forget your shoes; your feet are shapely –

but wear your green dress for me.

No: there's no need to speak.
So many words – so very many words
have flowed between us.
Just let the thoughts
find their own silences – and wear
your green dress for me, so you can feel
self-conscious enough to know
you are perceived as beautiful:

and if that knowledge should embarrass you – well,
I shall have to help you out of it – but first
just wear once more
your green dress,
once more for me.

Amoretti XXV – An Un-cruise Cruise

We've been together over thirty years,
and now you're seventy, we celebrate
in style: an un-cruise cruise on turquoise seas,
you snorkeling, or striding ahead
along a desert ridge. Our fellow passengers
take to you – of course they do.
The only down-side, that we have
twin beds, for though they make the space
more manageable, I cannot reach your hand
across that wide divide, or feel your warmth
or shape my shape to yours.
But now we have returned from holidays
I'll have you by me where I need you still
to hug you close, that you may know
my heart still beats for you as long ago.

Amoretti XXVI – Birthday Suit

This is your birthday – seventy no less.
When I first saw you in your birthday suit,
well, you were in your thirties and I had to look.
Behind you, a white waterfall, rowans
overhanging the narrow pool and, far above,
Blaven, which we had just climbed,
blue now in the late haze of the afternoon
and you, totally unselfconscious,
gracing the water with your slender form.
Well, I had to look again. But now
I also know the whole shape of your heart –
its truth and decency: for in your body and mind
there are no borrowings, the beauty is your own;
just as in nature what is meant to be
is what it is. So, though the hills we climb
are smaller now, the reddening rowans, the brown pool,
white waterfall, the mountain blue,
are still put to the test
to be as beautiful as you.

Amoretti XXVII – Not a Sonnet

Were these the only words that I could write
to wish you 'happy birthday' I still trust
that you would read between the lines, despite
their poverty of thought, and so adjust

your expectations and accept the love
they bear; for their defence is that they seek
to reach out, hand as though in sonnet glove
to find acceptance and so touch your cheek

with their affections, stilted though they be.
But they are not the only words that I
could write, nor this their only form, for see,
un-gloved, they join a flock of words which flies

with all the other Amoretti, far
beyond formalities, to celebrate
your birthday in wide, universal skies.

Amoretti XXVIII – Winter Solstice Work

You have spent all of the shortest day
repairing my old Arran Island sweater,
more holes than substance, islands in truth,
connected only by a slender isthmus here and there
of a stained strand of wool;
now, well into the dark, still patient and seemingly content,
you work on, needle-knitting joins and seams,
till my uncaring ways
are mended and the patches of existence
brought together and made one and whole.
This is winter solstice work, a kind of love
that comes from deep below
and far above.

Amoretti XXIX – This Much Endures

A childhood book; a family photographed
in black and white, their silent silhouettes
on the top of an island, wave goodbye to the west:
my sister's recollection and my own
shared through many years. My sister's dead.
The book, by whom I know not, and I know not where.

And now, near where we live our island life,
I see you on a ridge, your silhouette
a token of that memory re-lived,
and think, yes, this is it, it's true.
                              And yet
if others' dreams are our reality
then who is who and when is now and then?
It does not matter. This is my love for you,
my kind companion of these several years,
and, insofar as anything survives,
this much endures.

Amoretti XXX – I know You Will Approve

You are away – an ocean and a continent away,
visiting family. I take over your tasks. I feed the birds
who flit about the wall, wondering why their breakfast is so late.
Mine is smoked haddock in milk. I know you will approve.

The day demands my attention. The washing machine
must also be fed, the last load hung on the drier,
two items of yours a sudden intimacy. Outside, the cattle
mooch around hoping you'll come with scraps.

No luck. They turn away in undisguised disgust.
They know who I am, the one that clamps them in the yoke,
pierces their ears with tags and jams his bodyweight
against the calf's flank at castrations.

Time now to pressure-hose the pens.
I clear the peat ash, tip it down the slope,
gather more dross to keep the fire in overnight,
but the evenings have become a solitary vigil.

I am always wondering just what you might say,
learning to judge myself through you.
It seems we have slipped into each other,
are each other's thoughts, a mutual self-sufficiency.

We compete for which of us will be the first to die,
fearing the death of only one would break all contact
with the living world, the half survivor left alone
and paralysed with grief.

So it is good to keep our families close, to be in touch
with old and find new friends; for life
has its insistences - the birds will still need seed, the cattle
care and, above all, the fire kept alive.

Amoretti XXXI – Naiad's kiss

You come from the shower,
tall, slender-limbed, while I,
just woken, watch you in the light
of this spring morning streaming
through windows left un-curtained through the night.
As I shade my eyes
I call you to me and you cross the room,
come to the bed, naked and beautiful,
and lean to press your mouth on mine.
Your damp dark locks
trail wet across my face, your lips
emerging through a waterfall of hair
are sweet and liquid as they ever were -
and with this Naiad's kiss I drown once more.

DEDICATIONS

The Horses of Destiny – for Eva

I hear you from your earliest days
piping a nursery rhyme
to being part of the magical
Cunning Little Vixen,
you in the opera at Montpellier –
and now, a mother, singing
in your immaculate French
beside my daughter's piano
on which Romain searches out the harmonies.

It was not easy getting here.
Divided loyalties, seas and oceans crossed,
and always pain from a mis-constructed spine.
No one would know. You are poised and beautiful.
You, a native Scot, who can stand in any bar
in France and sing Brassens as to the manner born,
the band attentive to you, you to them.

And now you manage people and events
from your office, trusted
as is right. Your love, your tolerance,
your elegance, though never showing off,
and your calm ways with your little boys.

And thus the whirligig of time brings in
new life, new laughter,
as the horses of destiny rise and fall
and we no longer know who is astride,
who standing. Next time round
will you or I be there? Who knows?
But the music still revolves and I still hear
your singing from those earliest days
piping a nursery rhyme
as we go round and round.

A Storm of Decency
- for Paddy and Fiona Bushe

They never saw it coming
and nobody could have forecast it.
The weather men and the weather women
were all wearing the wrong clothes:

but the great thing about it was
that the oppressed and the forgotten
the humiliated and the hurt
the innocent and the loving

were all perfectly dressed for the event.
And what an event!

The Apocalypse had nothing on it
Judgement Day was a rained-off parade
Ragnarok was a ball game for mice
and the priests and the Doomsday men and the Doomsday
women

and the nay-sayers
and the cheats and the liars
and the torturers and the killers
and the war-mongers and most of the financiers with them

were all caught totally unawares
and swept right off their feet
and held upside down
until all the malice and wrong-doing

was shaken out of them
along with all filthy selfish thoughts
and petty demands
and hoarding habits

and all mean-mindedness
was blown away by a storm of decency.

How it came about
will never be known
but the old poets set aside their pens
and rejoiced
and the sun fell backwards with laughter
and then skipped across the heavens
to catch up on its duties
and the moon smiled for the first time
in its long serious life
and the stars all came to an agreement
and dropped down in the daytime
to smile in the eyes of children.

Your Profferred Cheek - for Dame Beryl Grey

Twice you have danced the role of Death,
and now, approaching ninety,
you speak of Death's authority,
your eyes smiling with absolute assurance.

On parting, as I reach
to kiss your proffered cheek
I have to steady myself, my hand
upon your firm slender waist.
You accept its presence there
as you have done
hundreds of hands in gestures
of strength, of beauty, and of tenderness.

Oh Death, I am smitten.
But when you stand at my bed-head
I will not ask that it be turned
to cheat you of your rights.
Instead, I will look up
and smile into your eyes
awaiting that last forever lift
high into weightless space.

For Alan Riach on the Occasion of his Sixtieth Birthday

When we approached the last bridge
and found it destroyed by the enemy,
many of us were tired, some sensing defeat,
gathered there, dubious, even perplexed,
viewing the dividing waters with cautious
circumspection, assessing the submerged rocks,
the treacherous eddies, the amorphous
fog on the other bank.

Would we, could we fight on?
The odds were ten to one against
and we had been fighting for
hundreds of years, through victories,
defeats, treaties and compromises;
and still they were there, grey;
an anonymous mist, unformed,
unformable.

But then there stepped forward from our ranks
a doughty red-haired warrior
who did not deign to turn for answer to his
"What are you waiting for, lads?" as he
strode straight into the great flood and,
with Byronic certainty, the current
sluicing round his thighs, held high
the sword of Intellect, heart-strong, the sun glinting
on its steely truth.

And so we followed on.

For Sheila, In Memoriam Leslie Henderson

When your widow asked for roses to be
bedded into soil, I asked in turn
that one such plant might be
the little white rose of Scotland:
for there was much of Scotland in you –
a hard metamorphosed spirit, multi-
coloured, often contorted, but utterly itself.
No compromises here; a geological
certainty, and a beauty determined
by realities – none harsher than those you faced
fighting a long slow retreat.
No comfort from Boethius there. If God
existed he would be, as my father once maintained,
a grey dispiriting creature. But it was you
who freed me from religion; probed with your scalpel mind
into the rotten sentiments, the shifty morals of the primrose path.
And so that little rose, clean-scented in critical mountain air,
recalls you to me now on the last lap of my race
and I am free to salute you in astonished retrospect
when what I am will yield all its alignments
and disperse – but not before I've penned
this single tribute to my first best friend.

Râg Shri in Glasgow – for Prakriti Dutta

It is the rich dark opening in the belly of your voice
which first alerts me to the danger I am in,
so visceral my whole skin primps itself
without command.

Around us, the huge deserted studio, empty
save for packing cases, a single chair,
a grand piano and its stool,
transforms into a heat-haze over desert plains;
far beyond, green forest rises into snow-capped peaks
higher than the clouds.

As your voice gently explores its middle range,
leaving blossoms trailing from every wall
and the floor strewn with petals,
the aroha of the râg rises, yearning,
your tongue as though in search of moisture
although moist itself. 'It is like,' you say,
'meeting with your lover. You really don't unfold yourself,
but you also want to show your beauty; so you can always feel
a hidden beauty inside this râg melody.'

All this blends like a miracle with
the sinuous line in Erik Chisholm's
Hindustani Concerto: the same râg rises
as a rippling ostinato breaks upon the shores
of his exotic music in gentle, urgent waves, until it all subsides
into a beautiful submission to, admission of
irresistible desire.

When you were here, you left behind
a little colourful Hindu god, legs folded,
mouth with serious expression
concentrating on his hands held out
clashing his cymbals. He is seated
on a window ledge and still protects the house
with loyal concentration.

But he is not as strong as your absence,
and your voice still travels through my being
from a land I've never seen; will never see.

Still That Girl - for Tüema at Eighty

Decidedly the prettiest creature I had ever seen,
not without mischief, even coquettishness
keeping at bay a string of eligibles:
but you were just another cousin to us
ready to dive at midnight off the end of the pier
and play with our own streams
of phosphorescent glory – you
memorable for your youthful elegance
and full of laughter and astonishment.
Your mother, beautiful indeed, your father
striking, debonair, gave you good genes,
sturdy opinions, disdain for obstacles.

I took a photo of you in a pretty dress,
and from your face, just slightly tilted, all the way down
past neckline, bodice, waist to frilly hem,
an edge of sunlight caught you, just as it did
the ragged stone of an old castle wall
which faced your youth with age.

Now age has you all right, no argument,
but you are still that girl, still
lovely, still determined and, what's more,
much more, to all that gentle artifice of
youth's allure you've added a true artistry,
finding the poet in yourself on board and canvas,
beauties harsh or sweet, drawing a blood line
of a different kind
flooding the arteries of the mind.

RLS for Sarah

This is a stone boat. Her name is RLS.
She is in the form of a leaf and her cargo is Imagination
which Davey Hume would call the Possible.
She is captained by her namesake
and they have sailed the seven seas.
She gives her love to lighthouses,
which is just as well, as, although she is made
of Skye green marble, she is in reality
a leaf, and therefore at the whim of the winds
who are not always thoughtful.
But she bobs and skims along,
thinks hurricanes are fun,
and loves to be tossed about at the hands of Fate.

If you wish to sail in this stone boat
you must suspend all kinds of disbelief, but,
with a cargo of Imagination
which Hume would call the Possible,
there should be no difficulty in the case.

For Tommy Gormley at Fifty

I'm lining up the shot;
two hands, fingers and thumbs at right angles
cutting out impedimenta, but the light -
the lighting isn't right. I need
a flood of intelligence from the left
a well-aimed spot of determination and
a balancing soft fill from the other side.
Nothing too obvious.
But it should be absolutely clear
what we are looking at:
not at all clear
what we are looking into.

Focus. The focus is too sharp.
Where are the soft edges? The sensitive bits?
No, no, no, no. We're not zooming in on this one:
there is always a context:
it doesn't matter that no-one
can read it, but we know
there are mountains and sea cliffs and
green glens and purple hills, and people, family,
moving about freely, laughing
and crying and fooling and loving.
We know they are there. They are all in the shot.
It's just that you can't make each one of them out.
But they are there and that is why
this can never be a close-up.

Nor is it a portrait; in the end
nothing and no-one in a single frame.

And so I've dropped my hands;
am searching now in seas
beyond the outer sound
where ships are dreams and dreams realities.

There, master of magic vessels, he'll be found.

A Consecration of the House
– for Margaret and John Hearne

There is grace in the grey granite wall
and in the flush pink flecked with grey; and over all
flat stars of mica waiting for the eye
to widen to the dusk of this stone sky
that, once a gable, houses now the hearth
to bind the fire in rock crystal earth,
and mark where you have drawn the curtain by
so that the stage of stars of yesterday
can cast new spells and star in a new play.

At the Tomb - for Scott Henderson

We were gathered round, the three of us,
like antiquarians speculating at the appearance
of this split-new carved stone slab.

Who ever commissioned such a tribute in our times?
hand-cut lettering, the uncials crisp as spear-heads,
a border of text almost obscured by woodbine.

The effigy was indeterminate of sex, the eyes
screwed shut as though contemplating
some intractable conundrum,

but the palms were splayed outwards
in a gesture of acceptance, and, of the feet, one
was raised a touch as though stepping out of the stone.

An old blind verger hobbled towards us,
one leg already sacrificed to the drink,
feeling his way with stick and crutch.

'Who is this person?' 'Aaah, it is the tomb
of the last eccentric. In the good old days
we bred them here before the market collapsed -

have you read the text?' 'We found it
indecipherable.' 'Well, I can read it for you
with my finger-tips, if you should wish.'

We wish. We wish with all our hearts.
We have searched the inscribed intricacies in vain.
'Please favour us with what it says.'

He kneels beside the raised bed of cold slate
and gently traces from the bottom left
right round the curving canopy of the top,

announcing as he reads all the way down
to bottom right, "We are indeed
a vile brood hatched from unlucky eggs."

Around the graveyard, the obligatory rooks
caw in derision as we three cast our eyes
downward and retreat beyond the wicket gate.

Gratias Ago Tibi – for Michael Purser

Well it was always you, thank God no other,
Who had to deal with being my Big Brother.
I never sensed your confessed animosity
And learnt a great deal from your generosity:
Especially when, as children, we played trains
Or built Meccano marvels, you were at pains
To teach me, patience rarely running thin.
And when we went on bicycles for a spin
At dark around the Glasgow west end lanes
We had such fun chasing one another
By torch beam in the smoggy sky
And you took the responsibility
Not only then, but later funded me
On my erratic musical journey.

One thing I hope I never made complain
That you were given the superior brain
And, though you have been wrong when I was right,
Our mental sparring has been all delight,
For sometimes you were right when I was wrong
And our debates were more like an old song
That sings beyond the edge of what it says.
And so, dear brother, also admired and loved,
There was no call for an apology
And though I cannot share in your doxology
I am content that when life finds an end
And we submit to something beyond creed
You will have been the nearest I'll concede
To someone I could name a true godsend.

Pussy Willow - for Becks Boyd-Wallis

When some old codger long ago
two thousand pages in
in his magnum op on willow trees
finally gave in

he wrote
– his final sentence you should note –

"They are indeed a puzzling tribe".

Now Becks, this is a serious issue
That can't be cleared like snot with tissue,
For willows are a genuine threat
To everybody's habitat,
For they're promiscuous beyond reason
And take no heed of place or season.

The ornamental willow has sex with the Japanese willow
The Japanese willow has sex with the river willow
The river willow has sex with the bank willow
The bank willow has sex with the meadow willow
The meadow willow has sex with the furry willow
The furry willow has sex with the marsh willow
The marsh willow has sex with the least willow
The least willow has sex with the heath willow
The heath willow has sex with the alpine willow

They all have furry excrescences
with which they pussy-powder the universe
into submission

and they are, for the most part,
quite useless.

MacCowan

It was a brutal night, an east wind cutting through the trees,
hail tearing the grass. All through the dark
you struggled to give birth, your muscles chilled
your calf reluctant to be born.

But we knew none of this, only you had not come
for hay at the first light. We found you down the hill,
standing beside your male calf lying limp on cold wet ground,
and you, unable to arouse him, no longer knowing what to do,
what could be done, experienced as you were.

I held the calf standing but he could not suck
and fell without my help to hold him up.

An hour to the surgery and back to fetch volostrum
and then I and my good neighbour, Katie,
pushed down the hill into the wind, and there you were
still standing, waiting, instinct alone holding you faithfully
to the bundle of wet bedraggled hide that lay
unmoving, waiting for its death.

And so we lifted him. I gripped his shoulders with my knees,
and held his muzzle high and pulled his cold-clenched teeth
open – but still he could not drink, not even when my neighbour
placed the teat between his lips to touch his tongue.

My head was bent touching his head; Katie bent too
as she dribbled the bottled milk into his mouth –
but even swallowing was beyond him, so weak he was with cold
and starved of oxygen from that long birth.

That's when you joined us, your rough tongue
licking the spilt volostrum from his cheek
while Katie massaged your calf's cold throat;
and, with our four heads, each touching each,
the cow, the calf, my neighbour and myself
became one thing, one life, determined.
Your long shapely horns never touched us;
only your coarse hair and the soft hair of the calf,
Katie's dark hair and my own. That's how it was.

That calf survived, as did you, dearest of all our cows;
patient and good; wise in your ways; a gentle leader, loyal.

Came the day when our dear Government decreed
that since you had been born before the outbreak of the BSE -
enabled by their own decisions - you must be slaughtered
and buried according to their book.

And so we took you to the Portree pens, my last sight of you
in the corner of a pen where you stood bewildered,
at a total loss, not knowing any longer where you were
or why I left you there. Your eyes haunt me.

I cannot cure this. I cannot make it good.
All I can offer to your memory,
this silly penance in a poem.

Kerry Races

My cousin's part-share in a nag
is the only reason I'm here.
But I know my great uncle could spot a winner
by the cut of her arse on the TV screen
even fifty years ago
and I am not to be outdone.
So I head for the paddock and the hard surface
of the ring.

The horses parade.
Front left, back right, front right, back left:
or the other way round. Whatever.
Suddenly I am hearing
difference.
Some strike the ground firmly: others tip-toe.
I know who gets my bet.
And then I watch the jockeys.
Anyone can steer a really good horse
to the winner's enclosure,
but if the odds are even,
put your money on the old boy,
still slim and light,
taut and sharp-eyed,
not without a certain weary wariness.
And the very man mounts on my cousin's bit of a horse
who strikes the ground with assurance
and I haste to the bookie's
and get 7:1. Not bad at all,
especially when she comes in.
Sometimes – just sometimes –
it pays to be a musician.

After the Races

I saunter up to the bar and stand beside
a figure in a check sports jacket
contemplating his drink. It is, I believe, spirits.
I order a Guinness and, as I wait,
fix my eyes on the gantry
behind the bar, but have to own to myself
that I chose to stand here, not further along.
My companion at the bar does not notice me.
He is, as I said, contemplating his drink.

Was it the jacket? No, it was the silk cravat
- a striking green beneath his orange hair.
I keep eyeing the gantry. I convince myself
he has the cravat pinned with a diamond clasp.
My drink arrives and I give it
due obeisance, until at last,
in our silent companionship,
I decide to speak.

The first, indeed the only thing I say to him is
'You look like a man who would have gold teeth.'
And he, delighted, turns to me,
and flashes a smile of total gold:
not a trace of ivory to be seen.

We return quietly to our drinks.
There is no need
for any further communication.